Hand Mending Made Easy

SAVE TIME AND MONEY REPAIRING YOUR OWN CLOTHES

Nan L. Ides

A Palmer/Pletsch PUBLICATION

Acknowledgments

In loving memory of my parents,
Adele and Martin Ides

And my grandmother
Frances Chaskes,
who was the strongest woman I have ever known.

Publisher's Cataloging-In-Publication Data
(Prepared by The Donohue Group, Inc.)

Ides, Nan L.
  Hand mending made easy : save time and money repairing your own clothes / Nan L. Ides ; photography by Michael Price and Pati Palmer ; illustrations by Kate Pryka.

  p. : col. ill. ; cm.

  Later edition of: Hand mending for beginners : 10 easy illustrated steps to save you time and money. Lincoln, NE: iUniverse, c2005.
  Includes index.
  ISBN: 978-0-935278-74-3

1. Clothing and dress--Repairing. 2. Sewing. I. Price, Michael, 1960- II. Palmer, Pati. III. Pryka, Kate. IV. Ides, Nan L. Hand mending for beginners : 10 easy illustrated steps to save you time and money. V. Title.

TT720 .I34 2008
646/.6

2008921113

Photography by Michael Price and Pati Palmer
Design and production by Linda Wisner
Illustrations by Kate Pryka
Copy editing by Ann Price Gosch

Copyright © 2008 by Palmer/Pletsch Incorporated.
Published by Palmer/Pletsch Publishing, 1801 NW Upshur Street, Suite 100, Portland, OR 97209 U.S.A.
Printed by Your Town Press, Salem, OR, USA

ISBN13: 9780935278743

Table of Contents

INTRODUCTION

What does it take to learn to hand mend?

Some thread, needle, pins,
a pair of scissors, a little patience and
practice, practice, practice!

You are rushing around in the morning to get ready for work or school and your hem rips or a button falls off.

What do you do?

Do you hurry up and change your whole outfit? NO!

1. Get out the needle and thread.

2. Take 2-3 minutes.

3. It's fixed.

Did you ever try on the perfect pair of pants, except they were just too long? No more putting them back on the rack or paying an extra $20.00 to have them hemmed. You'll be hemming them yourself soon enough.

This book will take you through several step-by-step processes of hand mending almost any garment. You will learn how to sew on the two different types of buttons, sew on a snap, hem a skirt and pants, and fix a ripped seam. There is even a full chapter on ironing and pressing tips, as well as a chapter on some very easy fashion changes that can be completed with the skills learned from this book.

You do not need a sewing machine to extend the life of your clothing. You just need to know how to mend—and to have the right tools. Saving money and time can begin with only a little sewing knowledge. By learning how to use a needle and thread, you can repair buttons, sew hems, restitch seams, do simple clothing alterations yourself, and more. There is no need to take your clothes to a tailor when you can do the mending quickly and easily at home.

This is not a "learn to sew" book. This is for the person who wants to save some money and not continue to take simple fixes to the tailor. It was written specifically for nonsewers, so you can understand the process and complete simple sewing fixes. This book is for everyone—children, adults, men and women alike. Everyone can learn to do basic hand mending.

There are many different ways to sew and fix garments. There are hundreds of types of stitches. This book will give you the best and most widely used solutions for each of the mending tips.

So before you get rid of a garment or take it the tailor's for an expensive bill, think of how much it costs to replace those clothes. Then compare that with the miniscule cost to mend them yourself.

Saving money is just a few stitches away!

SUPPLIES FOR HAND MENDING

The Basics

- ❏ pins
- ❏ needles—assorted package of sharps, sizes 5 (largest) to 10 (smallest)
- ❏ scissors
- ❏ measuring tape/ruler
- ❏ several basic colors of thread

    For basic hand mending, the 100% polyester or cotton-covered polyester thread found in most stores is sufficient. Most of the time, you should try to use thread that matches or is closest to the color of the fabric. This is especially important with hemming and mending an open seam.

- ❏ pencil or pen

Thread Tip:

Use thread a shade darker than the fabric, rather than lighter, if you are unable to match the fabric exactly. The slightly darker color will sew in to look as if it matches

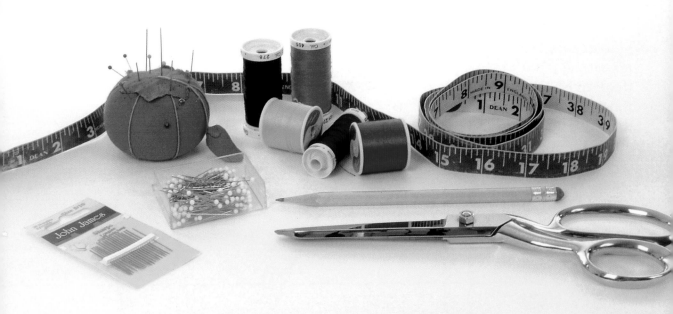

Nice-to-Have-Around Supplies:

- ❑ thimble
- ❑ hem gauge
- ❑ extra buttons and snaps
- ❑ needle threader
- ❑ a few extra needles
- ❑ embroidery needle
- ❑ magnetic pin holder
- ❑ tailor's chalk
- ❑ marking pen and pencil

Snap and Button Thread Tip:

Snaps are usually black or silver. Match the thread color to the fabric for silver snaps; black thread for black snaps.

For buttons, you really have a choice. Many buttons are for decoration as well as utility, so you can use matching or contrasting thread. In children's clothes, multiple thread colors are sometimes used as a fun accent.

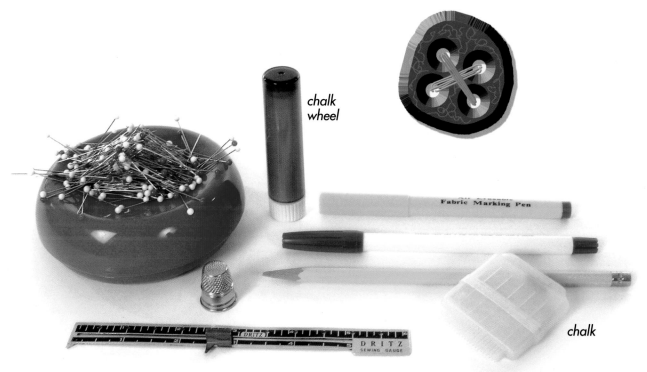

chalk wheel

Fabric Marking Pen

chalk

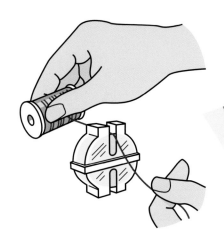

To keep your thread strong and tangle-free, run it through beeswax before you begin.

More Nice-to-Have-Around Supplies:

- ❏ ResQ Tape™
- ❏ beeswax (makes thread stronger)
- ❏ Fray Check™ (clear liquid that stops fabric from fraying)
- ❏ fusible web for hems and patches
- ❏ seam ripper
- ❏ Pinch-n-Pull Bodkin™ for pulling elastic through casings
- ❏ press cloth
- ❏ safety pins of various sizes
- ❏ full-length mirror

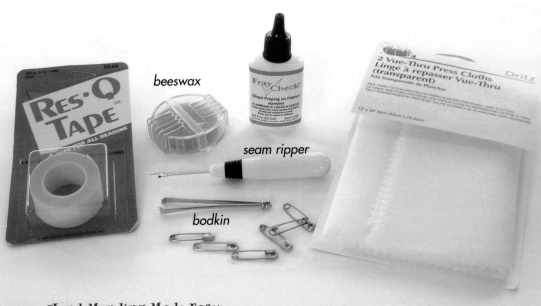

beeswax

seam ripper

bodkin

Where to get sewing supplies:

Hand sewing supplies can be purchased in these stores:

- ❏ fabric stores
- ❏ sewing machine/vacuum stores
- ❏ quilt shops
- ❏ craft stores
- ❏ dollar stores
- ❏ some drug stores
- ❏ some grocery stores
- ❏ some department-type stores

Does the Fabric Make a Difference?

There are hundreds of types of fabrics, but for basic mending, you just need to know the two basic categories: stretch and nonstretch. Knits are stretchy, as are some woven fabrics. There are many different types of stretch fabrics that are either two-way stretch (stretching horizontally across the body) or four-way stretch (stretching both horizontally and vertically). For this book, just know that if it's stretchy in any way, you'll need to adjust your hemming technique (see Chapter 5).

DEFINITIONS
(some words used in this book)

Basting – temporary long stitches to keep fabric in place

Casing – the "pocket" that contains elastic or a drawstring

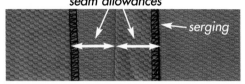

Eye of the needle – the hole where the thread goes through

Fusible web – a nylon mesh that melts with the heat of the iron. When put between two layers of fabric, it "glues" them together. It comes in rolls or by the yard.

Gather – drawing fabric fullness into a much smaller area

Hem depth – the amount of fabric folded up

Organic – natural

Pile/Nap – fabrics with a "fuzzy" surface, such as velvet and corduroy, and any fabric that may reflect the light differently from different angles.

Right side of fabric – the outside of the garment; the side of the fabric that faces out

Rip out – this does not mean to rip the fabric! Simply take out the existing stitching

Seam allowances – the width of the fabric between the edge and seam stitching

seam allowances ← serging

Serged/serger – a special machine finishes fabric edges by trimming them, then overcasting, as shown above

Shank – the loop on the back of certain buttons where the button is sewn to the fabric

Synthetic – manmade

Topstitch – stitching on the right side of the fabric through all layers, for example to hold a seam down to one side and/or for decoration

Wrong side of fabric – the inside of the garment

How Much Money Can You Really Save?

Average* charges for basic tailoring services:

Hemming:	straight	full/flared	lined (extra)
Pants	$12.00	$15.00	$3.00-$5.00
Skirt	$10.00	$15.00	$2.00-$3.00

	sewing	replacing & sewing
Buttons: (each)	$1.00-$2.00	$2.00-$3.00
Snaps: (each)	$1.00-$2.00	$2.00-$3.00

Fixing ripped seams:
Charges vary per garment, fabric, size of rip, and how difficult it is to maneuver the garment to repair the seam. Prices begin at $5.00-$7.00.

Pressing only:
Charges vary per garment size, length, and type of fabric.

Shirts	$ 5.00 and up
Skirt/pants	$10.00 and up

Sewing on a patch: (rare for a tailor to do this)
Prices usually begin at $12.00.

*These are average charges for urban-area tailoring services from a professional cleaner's business. Charges may vary per garment based on size and type of fabric.

CHAPTER ONE:

GETTING STARTED:
Threading a Needle

Supplies Needed:

❏ needle
❏ thread
❏ scissors

Threading a needle is the first step in any hand mending or sewing project. Practice it first using a needle with a large eye (hole). When you are ready to mend your garment, you can still use a needle with a larger eye as long as it easily slides through the fabric.

If you are unable to find thread that matches exactly, choose a thread that is a slightly darker shade than your fabric, because single threads will appear lighter when sewn. Cut a piece of thread approximately 18″- 20″ long. Longer thread will begin to fray (unravel) and tangle from going in and out of the fabric. It is also much harder to work with. Cut the thread with a good pair of scissors. Scissors do not need to be expensive; just make sure they cut and do not fray the thread.

Hold the thread between the thumb and forefinger about 1/4″ from the end of the thread so it is more stable when you put it through the eye of the needle. You may need to dampen the thread end (wet slightly by mouth) in order to make it pass through easily. Push the thread through the eye of the needle.

If a single thread (at right) will be used, you will knot only one end of the thread. Pull the thread through the eye far enough to create a tail of thread that is 3"–4" long. This end remains unknotted.

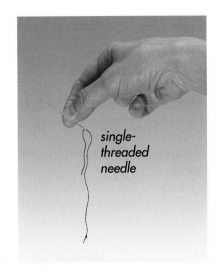

single-threaded needle

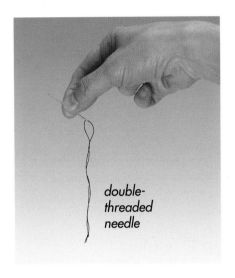

double-threaded needle

If double thread will be used (at left), pull the two ends of the thread together at the same length and and knot the ends together. (See page 16.)

When sewing, practice holding the needle between the thumb and middle finger with the fore-finger in front. The thumb and middle finger should be placed on the eye of the needle to keep the thread from slipping out as you stitch.

A single thread should be used where you do not want the thread to show and do not need the extra strength double thread offers.

Buttons: double thread
Snaps: double thread
Hemming: single thread
Fixing seams: single thread

But It's Really Hard to See!

Threading a needle is difficult if you cannot see up close. This probably includes most of us over the age of 40. Needle threaders can be used when you have difficulty threading a needle in the regular way. They are very inexpensive and can be purchased almost anywhere.

There are two types of needle threaders—a thin wire loop or a wire hook.

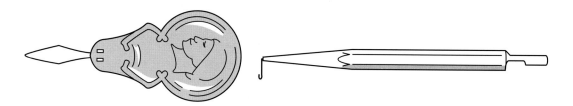

How to thread a needle with a wire loop threader:

Push the wire loop through the eye of the needle. Insert your thread into the loop. Pull the loop back out of the needle eye and your thread will come with it. It's that simple. If you do buy a needle threader, buy an extra one—they are very fragile and bend or break easily.

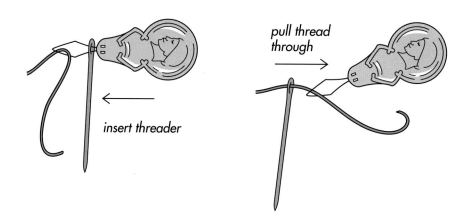

insert threader

pull thread through

How to thread a needle with a hook needle threader:

This was invented by a clever Australian and is available in sewing machine stores or from Palmer/Pletsch (page 78). Take the needle threader and push the hook through the eye of the needle. Hook a loop of thread and pull the needle threader and the thread back through the eye of the needle.

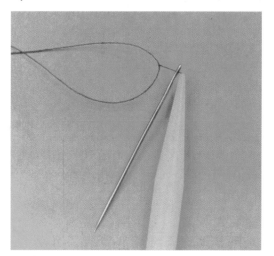 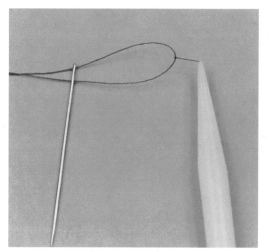

Thread Tip:

Use a thread 18"-20" long when hemming or doing other hand mending. Longer thread can knot, tangle or fray.

CHAPTER TWO:

Knotting the Thread

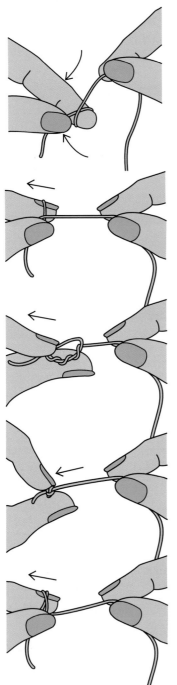

After threading the needle, take the end of the thread between your thumb and index finger. (If using a single thread, take one end of the thread to be knotted. If using double thread, take the two ends of the thread together.)

Supplies needed:

- ❏ needle
- ❏ thread
- ❏ scissors

Wrap the thread loosely around your index finger, continuing to keep the thread in place with your thumb. Dampening the forefinger will help.

While holding the other end of the thread taut, slide your index finger back along your thumb, twisting the threads together until the loop that is formed is pushed off the end of the index finger.

A loose knot should appear at the end of the thread. Slide the loop toward the end of the thread to form a tight knot.

If the thread pulls off your finger without forming a knot, try again and wrap the thread around your finger (not too tightly) a few more times.

Knotting the thread may take a little practice, but once you get it, it only takes a second.

Make sure the knot is large enough so it won't be pulled through the fabric. If it pulls through the fabric, repeat the knotting process, forming another knot on top of the first knot.

If the knot is not at the end of the thread, simply cut off the remaining thread close to the knot.

You will also need to make a knot at the end of your stitching, which will be explained in the next chapter.

You are now ready to mend.

Sanity Tip:

To save time and frustration in an emergency, always keep one or two needles threaded with black and/or white thread.

CHAPTER THREE:
Stitching Basics

- Hold the needle between your thumb and index finger and use the middle finger to push it through the fabric.

- Hold the fabric over the index finger of the other hand with your thumb on top.

- Sew from right to left if you are right-handed or from left to right if you are left-handed.

- Use a single thread unless you need extra strength, then use it doubled (see page 13).

- Work with smooth, even motions to keep thread from tangling. Draw the thread all the way out after every stitch so no loops will form.

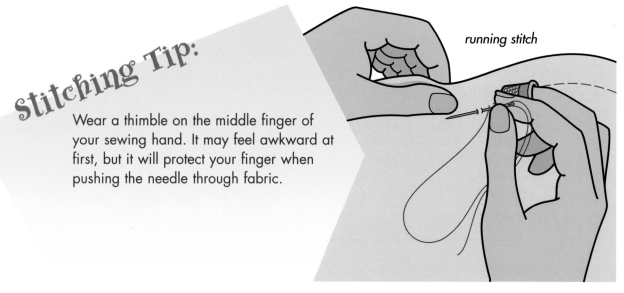

running stitch

Stitching Tip:

Wear a thimble on the middle finger of your sewing hand. It may feel awkward at first, but it will protect your finger when pushing the needle through fabric.

Knot the Thread at the End of Stitching

When you get near the end of your thread, or you are at the end of your stitching, you need to knot the thread. Stop stitching when your thread is still 3"- 4" long. You need to have this length to form a knot.

You can knot the thread in one of two ways:

- With your needle on the wrong side of the fabric, take a tiny backstitch and pull the thread, leaving a small loop. Insert the needle and thread through the loop. Pull the thread to close up the loop at the base of your stitches. One knot should be fine, unless the fabric is very loosely woven or knitted. Then make a few knots on top of each other.

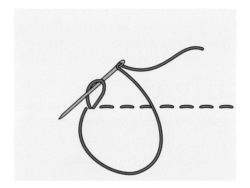

- If you are working with a double thread, you may use the method above or knot the two strands together. With your needle on the wrong side of the fabric, cut the thread at the needle eye. Now you have two even strands of thread. Separate the strands and tie a simple knot close to the fabric. If you wish, make a few knots and then clip the thread about 1/4" away from the knot.

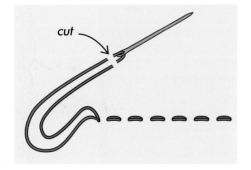

cut

CHAPTER FOUR

Closures/Fasteners

The most common closures are buttons, snaps, and hooks and eyes. Some can be decorative and add to the appearance of the garment. To close and fasten most garments, one edge of the opening laps over the other. On women's garments the right side laps over the left; men's garments lap left over right. Fasteners have two parts—one part is sewn to the underlap, the other to the wrong side of the overlap.

Supplies Needed
- ❏ needle
- ❏ thread
- ❏ button(s), snaps, hooks and eyes, frogs
- ❏ scissors
- ❏ pins

Buttons

Buttons come in many shapes and sizes, but there are really only two types of buttons.

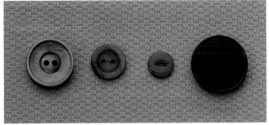

- ■ Buttons with holes—usually two or four holes.

- ■ Buttons with a shank—the little loop that hangs off the bottom of the button.

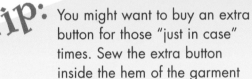

shank

Buy a Replacement Button

Buttonholes are sewn to match the size of the button. When buying a new button(s), take the old one and/or the garment with you to the store for sizing. Try to match the button if there are several. Otherwise, replace all the buttons. Buttons can be purchased in many places nowadays. The largest variety will be offered in sewing or craft stores.

Tip: You might want to buy an extra button for those "just in case" times. Sew the extra button inside the hem of the garment or onto an inside seam.

Mark the Button Position

If a button is being replaced or changed, first button the garment and mark with two pins (crisscrossed) exactly where the button should go. Many times the thread from the old button is still in place and can be used as a marker and removed after the button is sewn back on.

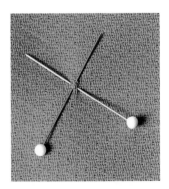

Prepare Your Needle and Thread

Always use double thread when sewing on buttons. Thicker threads are also useful, such as topstitching or upholstery thread. Use thread as close to the button color or garment color as possible. If replacing one of several buttons, match the thread used in sewing the other buttons. Remember to knot the thread (both ends together) before beginning to sew (see page 16).

Sewing On Buttons with Holes

Look at the other buttons on your garment. Do they have two holes or four? If there are four holes, are they sewn with two parallel lines of thread or crisscrossed? It does not matter if threads are crisscrossed or parallel, but they should be consistent.

Two Holes

Begin by pushing the threaded needle through the wrong side of the fabric in the middle of the marked area to the right side. Hold the button between the thumb and forefinger of your left hand (or right hand, if you are left-handed) and pull the needle and thread up through the first hole of the button. Put the needle down through the other hole and into the fabric to the back. Do this several times.

Four Holes

Stitch back and forth through two holes on one side of the button (horizontally or vertically), and then repeat for the two holes on the other side. Or crisscross the two rows of stitching.

To knot the thread, see page 19.

 Do not pull the stitches too tight. All buttons need enough give on the thread so that the button does not pull on the fabric when it is buttoned.

Sewing On Buttons with Shanks

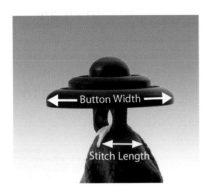

For illustration purposes, the fabric is pulled down to show where to stitch. When sewing, do not stretch the fabric like this; let it lie flat.

What is a shank? The shank of a button is the small piece that hangs down underneath the button—the part the needle and thread will go through to attach the button to the garment.

Insert the needle into the fabric from the wrong side at the button marking. Pull the needle and thread all the way through. Hold the button in place on the fabric with your left hand (or right, if you are left-handed). Insert the needle through the shank and back into the fabric to the wrong side. Repeat several times.

How long should the stitches be? The stitch length is the measurement from bringing the needle up through the shank and back down into the fabric. It should be about one-half to three-fourths the diameter (width) of the button.* For example, if the button is 1" in diameter, the stitches should be at about 1/2"-3/4" long.

All shank buttons will wobble a bit, but the longer the stitches, the more secure the button will be.

*Buttons are measured in diameter/width, stitches are measured in length.

Create a Thread Shank on a Button with Holes

For thick fabrics, such as coats, add a shank to a button with holes. It's very easy and your garment will hang more smoothly.

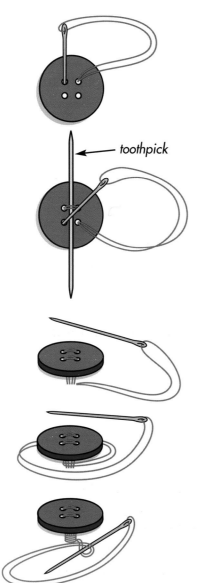

toothpick

1. Use a double-threaded needle. Knot the thread and take a stitch at the button marking. Bring the needle and thread through one hole in the button. Center the button over the stitch. Pull the thread all the way up.

2. Insert the needle into one of the holes of the button. Place a toothpick (or a thick needle or pin) along the center of the button between the holes. This will create slack for a shank to be formed. Go down through the other hole and back into your fabric.

3. Take 3 or 4 stitches through each pair of holes.

4. Bring the needle to the right side just under the button and remove the toothpick.

5. Wrap the thread 2 to 3 times around the button stitches to form the shank.

6. Secure the thread by knotting. (See page 19.)

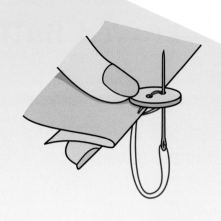

An easy way to create a shank is to fold the fabric back where you want to sew on the button. Place the button over the fold with the holes the same distance from the fold as the length of the shank you want.

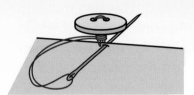

After stitching through the button and fold several times, wrap the thread around the stitches to form a shank. Knot the thread in the fold.

Sewing On More Than One Button

If sewing on multiple buttons, check the position of each button after it is sewn on. Do not wait until all of the buttons are sewn. If one is a little misaligned, then they all could end up being a little off, making the garment hang unevenly or pull.

Buttons in Waistbands

Sometimes waistbands of pants or skirts have buttons on the inside. When sewing on a button on the inside, make sure that you do not stitch all the way through the waistband so that the thread shows through on the right side. Sew the button on by taking tiny stitches through several threads of the fabric instead of going all the way through the thickness of the band.

Repair a Frayed Buttonhole

Sometimes the threads of a buttonhole will fray and break. You have two options for repairing this:

The quick fix if all the threads are still there, but frayed:

Place a dab of Fray Check along the frayed area. This will make the buttonhole somewhat stiff when dry, but might be fine for a small area. Test on the fabric first to make sure the fabric color does not change.

OR sew a tiny blanket stitch:

Match your thread to the existing buttonhole thread. Using a double threaded needle, take tiny stitches very close together to cover the frayed area. (See blanket stitch, page 56.)

Snaps

Snaps are sewn on entirely differently than buttons.

Test the snap before sewing it on; open and close it a few times to make sure that it fits together snugly, but not so tight that the garment may be ripped when trying to undo it.

Snaps have two halves—the ball and the socket. The ball half is thinner and has a short extension that fits into the socket half of the snap. The ball is less bulky than the socket so it is usually sewn to the underside of the overlap of the garment.

Supplies Needed

- ❏ needle
- ❏ thread
- ❏ snap(s)
- ❏ scissors
- ❏ pins

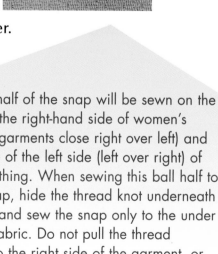

ball half   socket half

Mark the Snap Position

Close the garment and mark with pins (with an X) or tailor's chalk exactly where the snap should be sewn.

Prepare Your Needle and Thread

Use double thread or very heavy thread. Thread the needle, then knot the thread, both ends together.

Sewing On the Snaps

1. Take a stitch on the inside of the garment where the snap will be placed.

   Begin with the ball half (the ball half is sewn on with the extension pointing up; the socket half is sewn with the hollow/hole facing up).

Tip: The ball half of the snap will be sewn on the inside of the right-hand side of women's clothing (garments close right over left) and the inside of the left side (left over right) of men's clothing. When sewing this ball half to the overlap, hide the thread knot underneath the snap and sew the snap only to the under layer of fabric. Do not pull the thread through to the right side of the garment, or the stitches will show.

2. Draw the needle through just a few threads of fabric on the underside and bring it up through one of the holes of the snap. Take several stitches through the hole, catching just a few threads of fabric each time. Do not go through all layers or the thread will show on the outside of the garment.

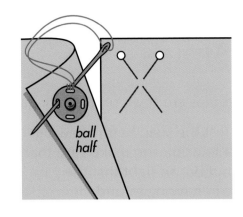

ball half

3. Finish with one hole before going to the next.

4. Now run the needle under the snap, picking up a few strands of the fabric. Go to the next hole and do the same thing.

5. When you have sewn through all four holes of the ball half of the snap, knot the thread, making sure the knot is very small. Bring the needle and thread under the snap to hide the knot, and clip the thread. Before sewing on the socket half of the snap, once again try on the garment or just close it and double-check the marking for the other side of the snap. Mark very carefully.

Sew the socket half of the snap the same way as the ball half, but with the hollow of the snap facing up.

socket half

Once both sides of the snap are sewn, check once more for fit.

After the ball half is sewn on, lap the garment layers as they will be worn. Insert a pin through the layer with no snap and poke it through the hole in the center of the ball half. Separate the layers and place the socket half of the snap on the pin.

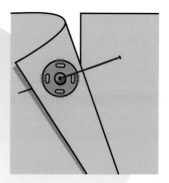

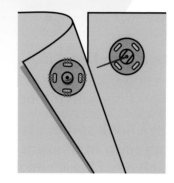

Sewing On More Than One Snap

When sewing on multiple snaps, check the position of each snap after you sew it. Do not wait until they are all sewn on. If one is a little misaligned, then they all could end up being a little off, making the garment hang unevenly or pull.

Hooks & Eyes

Hooks and eyes are hidden fasteners. They can be used to hold edges butted together or overlapped. Hooks and eyes are available in several sizes and colors, but usually you'll find them in black or silver.

Supplies Needed

- ❏ needle
- ❏ thread
- ❏ hook & eye
- ❏ scissors
- ❏ pins or chalk

No-sew hooks and eyes that clamp into the garment are available, but the hooks and eyes that you would usually be replacing are sewn into place. They come with either loops or straight eyes.

Sewing on a hook and eye is very similar to sewing on a snap. The stitches are sewn from inside the hole to outside the hole. The traditional type of hook and eye usually is sewn on the top edge of a zipper on pants, dresses or tops. It can also help hold the fabric in place on diagonal wrap-front necklines.

Begin with the hook piece. Thread the needle with double thread. Knot the thread. As with buttons and snaps, you need to mark the area very well; or keep the threads attached from the hook and eye that you are replacing. Pull the thread up from the inside of the garment and through one of the holes of the hook. Insert the needle right outside the hole and then up through the hole again and down on the outside. Continue this way, almost "wrapping" the hole 3-4 times. Then go to the second hole and take 3-4 stitches.

 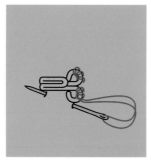

Now secure the top of the hook by stitching it to the fabric just under it. Do not stitch all of the way through to the right side of the garment. Knot the thread when done. (See page 19.)

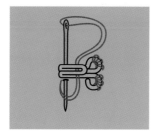 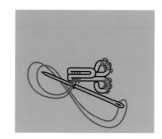

Now, sew the eye piece. Use a pin to mark where the middle needs to be. Sew through the holes at each end just as you did for the hook.

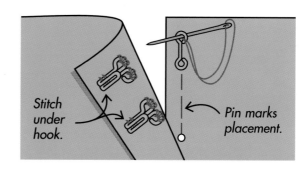

Stitch under hook.

Pin marks placement.

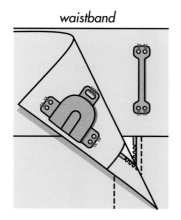

waistband

Use a larger hook and eye for a waistband, as shown to the left. The larger hook piece will be sewn onto the inside of the waistband that overlaps. Thread a needle with double thread and knot the thread. Bring the thread up through one of the holes and down on the outside of the hole.

Do not pull the thread all the way through the waistband because it would then show on the right side of the band. Mark the placement of the "eye" on the underlap of the waistband and sew it into position through all layers.

A NOTE ABOUT NO-SEW HOOKS: Some hooks on ready-to-wear are not sewn on; they are attached to the garment by sharp prongs, which are then turned under. If the waistband is even just slightly tight, this type of hook starts to pull out of the fabric. Replace them with hooks that are sewn on.

Make an "Eye" Out of Thread

Thread eyes are often used at the top of a dress zipper and often break. Use a single strand of thread and knot the end.

1. Take a stitch the length you want your "eye" to be.

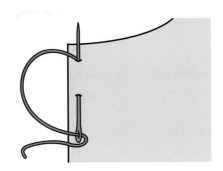

2. Take three more stitches the same length in the same location. These will be your core threads.

3. Next take a tiny stitch in the fabric at one end of your threads. Make a blanket stitch over the thread core with the stitches close together until you reach the other end. (Make sure you don't catch the garment fabric as you sew.) Secure the thread. (See page 19.)

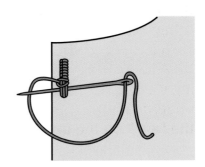

Note: These illustrations are enlarged views. The actual thread eye would be approximately half this size.

A Decorative Closure with a Frog

A very popular decorative fastener is the frog, especially in Asian-style clothing. Frogs come in numerous colors and consist of two pieces, the loop and the ball.

photo courtesy of The McCall Pattern Company

To Sew On a Frog

Pin the ball of the frog in place on the left side of the garment, positioning the ball halfway over the edge of the fabric or slightly to the left, whichever you prefer. Pin the loop onto the right side. Use a single-threaded needle in the same color thread as the frog. Knot the thread. Bring the threaded needle up from the wrong side of the fabric. Tack each loop of the frog down, hiding the stitches underneath the frog.

Note: The stitches in the illustration are exaggerated. The stitching should be underneath the frog where it does not show.

Zipper Fixes

Zipper Stitching

Sometimes the stitching wears out at a stress point on a zipper. Pull any loose ends to the wrong side and tie them, if possible, to prevent any further unstitching. Then sew on the previous stitching line with a double thread in a matching color, using a backstitch (see page 46).

Missing Teeth

If a tooth is missing from a separating zipper (one that separates into two parts, like the front of a jacket), or from the upper part of a non-separating zipper, the zipper needs to be replaced. That is too big a job for hand mending. But if a tooth is missing near the bottom of a non-separating zipper, the zipper can be rescued. Zip the zipper until the pull is above the missing tooth. With a double-threaded needle, take several stitches around both rows of teeth, to make a new bottom stop.

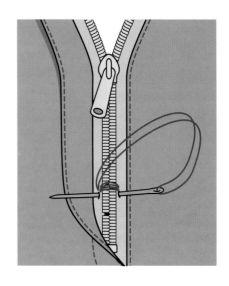

A tip for a pull that won't stay up:

If the pull of a coil zipper slides down and won't stay zipped anymore, there is an easy solution. Squeeze gently with a pair of needle-nosed pliers on the square bottom end of the zipper pull, on both sides of the center bar, bringing the front and back of the pull slightly closer together.

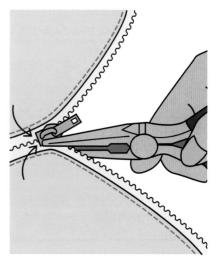

CHAPTER FIVE:

Hemming

Almost all garments have a hem. Fixing a hem is a mending chore everyone will need to do at one time or another.

If you are not experienced at hand stitching, your first few hems may have uneven stitches, but that's okay as long as the stitches do not show on the right side of the garment. In thinner fabrics, the stitches may leave tiny indentations, but the thread itself should not show. With practice, you'll be able to master hemming in any fabric.

Supplies Needed

- ❏ needle - Use the finest needle you can thread. Remember, the smaller the needle, the smaller the hole. Use that needle threader!
- ❏ thread
- ❏ scissors
- ❏ measuring tool(s)
- ❏ writing utensil
- ❏ pins
- ❏ iron (and press cloth)

There are several steps to hemming, but all are very easy.

The steps here are for the basic hemming process. For details on various special hemming situations, see pages 42-44.

Prepare for the New Hem Length.

1. If changing the hem of a garment, use a seam ripper or a good pair of small sharp-pointed scissors to "rip out" (take out) the old hem. Take care not to make any holes in the fabric when you take out the thread. (See step 7 on the next page for an example of when you could skip this and the next step.)

2. Press out any crease lines. (See Chapter 11 for pressing how-tos.) If you are lengthening the garment, you want to be sure the crease line will disappear. If shortening, any remaining crease line will show only on the inside of the garment.

3. Now figure out the length you want your garment to be. The best way to do this is simply to try on the garment in front of a full-length mirror. Stand on a hard floor and have the shoes on that will be worn with the garment.

Turn under the hem to where you think you might like it and pin it in place. It may take a few tries—pinning and unpinning—testing different lengths to get the right garment length.

Sometimes it's easier to stand on a stool.

Note: If a skirt or dress hem is uneven, have a friend measure from the floor with a yardstick and place pins the same distance all the way around.

4. Once you know the length you want, place pins every 2"-3" on the right side of the garment in the exact place where the hem will be folded up. Tailor's chalk can also be used, but first test it on an inconspicuous part of the fabric to ensure that it won't leave any permanent marks.

5. Remove any pins that are holding the hem up.

6. Determine the hem depth. It will vary with the amount of flare.

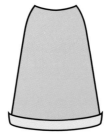

Straight skirts and pants can have deeper hems—1¾"- 2". The weight will help them hang better.

Slightly flared skirts and pants need a narrower hem width—1¼"-1½"—so you will not have too much to ease in at the top edge of the hem. (See page 42.)

Very full skirts and soft fabrics or stretchy knits are best with a narrow hem, 1/4"-1" or 1/8" turned under twice and hand rolled.

7. Measure down from the pins the amount you want for a hem allowance and mark with chalk. Trim away excess fabric. If you are changing the hem quite a bit you may be able to cut the entire original hemmed portion of the garment away but If you are changing it only a small amount you may have to remove the original hem stitching first to create a large enough hem allowance. (See steps 1 and 2.)

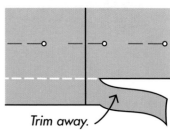

Trim away.

8. If you are shortening the skirt or pants, trim the seam allowances in the hem allowance to 1/4" to reduce bulk.

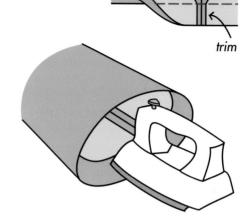

trim

9. Remove pins and press the new hem from the inside. Be careful not to press over the cut edge of the hem. You'll get a ridge on the right side. To protect the fabric while pressing, use a press cloth. (See page 60.)

10. Using the hem fold line you have pressed, pin the hem up all around, using as many pins as needed to keep the hem in place. Try on your garment once more to check the length and to make sure it is all even. (Skirt hems should always be the same distance from the floor all the way around, except if the hem was originally designed to be uneven.) Take off the garment and turn inside out.

11. Using the same pins from the step above, move them down to about 1/4" above the fold line.

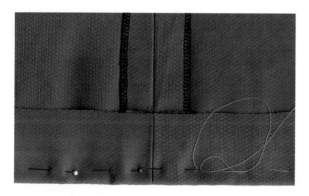

You can use pins or long basting stitches to hold the hem in place before sewing. Basting stitches are done with any contrasting color thread, taking long stitches that will easily pull out after the hem has been sewn and before it is pressed. The thread is not knotted.

Finish the hem edge to prevent raveling.

You need to make sure the hem edge won't ravel.

You could hand sew seam binding on top of the edge.

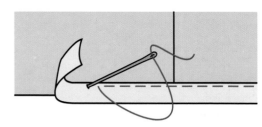

OR

You could hand overcast the raw edge.

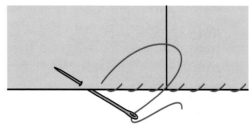

OR

fold under the raw edge at the top of the hem.

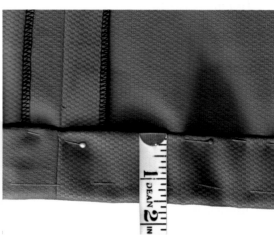

Tip: For knits, there is no need to turn under the edge because a knit will not ravel. See Designer Hem Stitch, page 40.

Now It's Time to Sew the Hem

Two stitch types are described on the next two pages, one for when the raw edge is turned under and the other for when it isn't and you need an "invisible" hem.

Tip: When you are sewing a hem, it is easiest to lay the garment flat on a table or on your lap. If laying the garment flat on your lap, be careful not to catch the clothes you are wearing into your stitches (this happens to everyone!).

Slipstitch: Use when you have turned under the raw edge.

1. Using matching or slightly darker thread, thread a needle and knot using single thread (see page 16).

2. Work from right to left (unless you are left-handed) with a single thread. Secure the knotted thread inside the hem.

3. Pull the needle and thread through the fold of the hem, close to the folded edge, from the underside to the top. This way the knot will be hidden under the hem.

4. About 3/8" away, pick up just a few threads of the garment directly above the folded edge. You should be picking up just a few fibers of fabric for each stitch. If too many threads are picked up, your stitch will show on the right side of the garment. Also, leave a little slack in your thread because pulling the stitches too tightly will make the hem show on the right side.

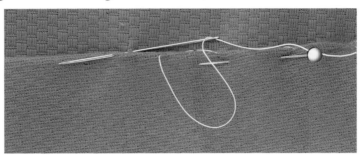

5. Take another stitch through the folded fabric. Your stitches should not show much on the inside and should be almost invisible on the outside.

6. Continue to run the needle under the fold of the hem, coming up through the fold, and take tiny stitches (strands) through the garment just above the folded edge. Work your way along the hem, making the stitches as invisible as possible on the right side. Practice to get a good, strong stitch and the look you want on the outside of your garment.

7. Lay the garment down and finger press the hem flat to make sure everything is lying very smoothly.

8. Knot the thread close to the fabric as shown on page 19. Cut off the remaining thread.

Designer Hem Stitch: Use when you don't turn under the edge and want a truly invisible hem.

This stitch is invisible on any fabric. Finish the raw edge of the hem if the fabric ravels (page 38). Use a single strand of thread and the finest needle you can thread, like a size 10 sharp.

1. Fold back the hem edge about 1/2".

2. Take long, loose stitches catching only a single fiber of the outside of the fabric.

3. Every few stitches, pull or stretch hem horizontally to loosen stitches and then secure by knotting in the hem allowance. This will protect the hem in case you accidentally step into it.

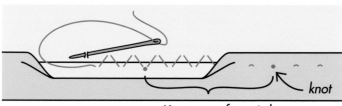

Knot every few stitches.

Secure the Thread Ends

To secure the thread at the end of a row of stitching or when a new strand of thread is needed, simply knot the thread and tuck the end into the hem of the garment.

Another way to knot the thread is to stitch in the same place a few times, going through the same thread loop.

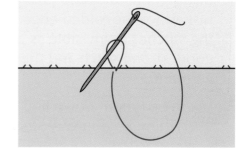

When you run out of thread in the middle of stitching a hem (remember, your thread should not be longer than 18"-20"), restart your stitching about an inch before where you left off. This overlap will make the hem extra secure just in case the knot pulls through.

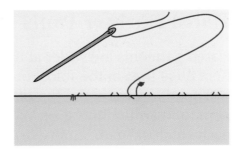

Congratulations!
You have just sewn your first hem!

You just saved at least $10.00, if not more!

Special Hemming Situations

Pant Hems That Are Longer in the Back

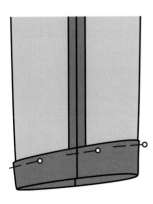

Pant legs come in all different widths. With certain widths and shoes, it may look better to have the back hem slightly longer than the front, but no more than a total of 1" difference. This is how many men's trousers are hemmed. To do this, fold up the center front of each leg in the middle to the finished length. Then fold up the center back of the pant legs so they are a little longer. Fold up the rest of the pant hem, tapering from front to back to make a smooth hem edge.

Flared Skirts or Pants

Flared garments are wider at the hem edge than at the fold. You will need to ease in the top of the hem to fit around the skirt. With each stitch, take up some extra fabric, as if gathering. Only tiny bits of fabric should be gathered at each stitch. Try to even the gathers all around the garment hem. Narrowing the depth of the hem to about 1" makes this easier. Also, place pins very close together on the bottom edge of the garment to keep the hem in place or use a long basting stitch just above the bottom fold instead of using pins. Remove basting once the hem is finished.

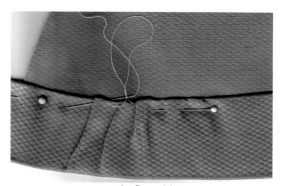

*too-wide flared hem —
gather fabric with each hemming stitch*

Tapered Skirts, Pants, and Sleeves

Tapered garments are narrower at the bottom edge. You will need to open the seam in the hem area and let it spread until the fabric lies smooth. Also, turn under the sides of the split seam and slipstitch (see page 39) the edges to the seam allowances, being careful not to have the stitches go through to the right side of the garment.

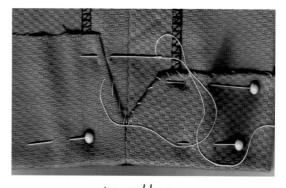

*tapered hem —
split seam in hem and stitch down*

Linings

Linings should be hemmed exactly the same as the hem, except the lining should be 1"-2" shorter than the garment. Hems in linings face opposite the outside hem — meaning that the insides of both the garment and the lining face each other.

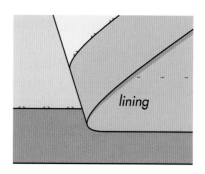

lining

Hemming Leather/Suede Pants, Skirts or Unlined Jackets

This is probably the easiest of all hems—because you do not need to sew. Leather hems are actually glued with special glue. The glue can usually be found in craft stores, sewing stores, possibly even at your local shoemaker's, and is inexpensive. Make sure it is meant for leather. Ordinary craft glue may dry very hard and crack and the hem will fall down. Leather glue allows the fabric to move without cracking.

Simply follow these steps for preparing a hem:

Measure how much needs to be hemmed up. Leather garment hems should be about 1½"-2" wide. The edges do not need to be turned under or finished because leather/suede will not fray. Before you glue, make sure the garment is the correct length. You can use masking tape to hold the hem up. (Other tape may leave marks or residue on the fabric, especially on suede.) Pins may leave small holes or indentations in the leather. Once the glue is on the fabric, it is very difficult to remove. Always test a dab of the glue on the piece you cut off or on an inside seam allowance to make sure that it does not discolor the leather/suede.

Using the manufacturer's instructions, use a minimal amount of glue and press down on the hem. You can use pieces of masking tape to keep the hem in position until it dries.

Fused Hem

Fusible web is a nylon mesh that melts with the heat of the iron. When put between two layers of fabric, it "glues" them together. It comes in rolls or by the yard. Use it for a very fast hem on heavier fabrics where it won't show through. It is permanent, so be sure you have the garment length you want. Cut a strip of fusible web 1/4" narrower than the hem width. Place it near the fold and turn up the hem allowance to cover it. Press with a steam iron 10-15 seconds to melt the web.

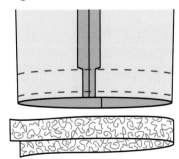

Emergency Hem Fixing

Don't have a needle and thread available? In an emergency, use a double-sided tape like Res-Q tape. The tape will not last very long; it should be used only for a short period of time. Also, always remember to remove the tape before washing or dry cleaning the garment.

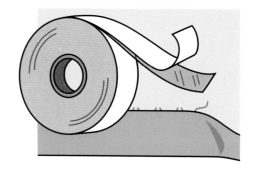

Curtains

Ever find the perfect curtains for your home, but they were way too long for your windows? Well, here is another place you can use your new hemming skills. Follow the directions for preparing, cutting, and hemming a garment. As with all hemming, measure the curtain length carefully. Curtain hems are usually much deeper than garment hems, because the deeper hem helps weigh down the curtain to hang better. A curtain hem can be 5"-6" deep, depending on the length of the curtain or drapery, so you may not need to cut off any fabric.

CHAPTER SIX:
Fixing Ripped Seams & Holes

Supplies Needed

- ❏ needle
- ❏ thread
- ❏ scissors

Ripped Seams

It's frustrating to find a hole or tear in one of your favorite garments, especially right when you plan to wear it, but often you can fix the rip or hole with simple mending or patching. If you have never done this before, don't fear; it's not as hard as it sounds.

Fixing broken seam stitching by hand can be very simple, although there are a few seams where a rip should be fixed with a sewing machine. This includes when cross seams have ripped open, such as the underarm and sleeve seams or sleeve and shoulder seams.

The type of edge finishing determines how the seam will be mended. There are several types of seam allowance edge finishings. Following are the four most popular:

seam allowance edges serged together

seam stitching

seam allowance edges serged together

topstitching

seam stitching

Seam A

The seam is sewn and the seam allowances are pressed to one side and "serged" together with a special sewing machine (serger) that sews an overlock stitch. The serger trims the edges and overcasts them in one operation. Most seams are finished this way.

Seam B

Same as A but also topstitched about 3/8" from the seam (jeans, khakis, etc.). This is a strong seam that normally will not rip open.

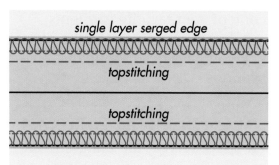
single layer serged edge

Seam C

The seam is sewn and pressed open and each edge is serged, or, if the garment is lined or the fabric isn't ravelly, left as is.

single layer serged edge

topstitching

topstitching

Seam D

The seam is sewn, seam allowances are finished, and then the seam is pressed open and topstitched down (rare; decorative).

For Seams A and C, use the backstitch:

A backstitch is the strongest of the hand stitches. It looks much like machine stitching—even stitches with very little space between them. Since you are working on the inside of your garment, you do not need to hide the thread knots.

1. Turn the garment inside out and find the broken stitches.

Note: In the illustrations that follow, the serged edges of the seam allowances are not shown. The thread in the needle is a different color for illustration clarity only.

2. If you are working with Seam C, bring the seam allowances together. If you are working with Seam A, the two seam allowances will already be together.

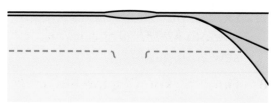
End here.   Begin here.

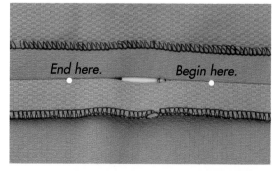

3. Thread a needle with a single strand of matching or slightly darker-colored thread. Knot the thread. Begin in the original stitching line approximately 1" to the right of where the seam is ripped.

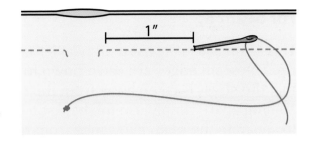

4. Bring the needle out of the fabric about 1/8" to the left in exactly the same line of the original stitches and pull the thread through.

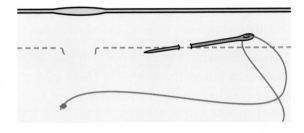

5. Place the needle back 1/8" into the original hole next to the knot and come out of the fabric 1/8" to the left of where the thread emerges from the fabric.

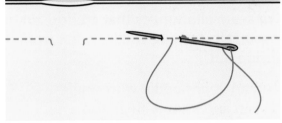

Note: Smaller or larger stitches may be taken, if desired.

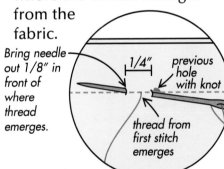

Bring needle out 1/8" in front of where thread emerges.

1/4" previous hole with knot

thread from first stitch emerges

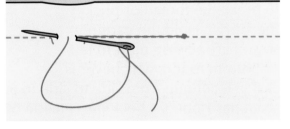

6. Continue sewing, each time going 1/8" backward and a 1/4" forward, to about 1" beyond the ripped section.

7. Do not pull the thread too tight; you want the resulting seam to be smooth and free of puckers. As always, practice the stitch before you sew your garment.

8. Finish by knotting the thread. (See page 19.)

For Seam B:

This seam is usually used on heavier fabrics such as denim, which rarely rip. The seam edges are sewn down for decorative purposes, but also so that the stress is taken away from the seam area. If the seam does start coming apart, simply use the backstitch to mend it. You will not be able to separate the seam allowance from the garment; therefore, carefully pick up only a few fibers of the fabric instead of going all the way through to the right side of the garment. This will be much easier in denim.

Make sure that you follow the old seam line exactly and that the thread does not show through on the right side of the fabric. Using the exact color or slightly darker thread will help keep the thread hidden.

For Seam D:

For seam allowances that are topstitched, fixing a rip is also very easy. Again, all stitching will be done from the inside, so turn your garment inside out.

Thread your needle with single thread and knot it. Begin on one side of the seam about 1" from where the seam began to rip and take very tiny stitches from one side to the other, pulling tight (but not too tight to break the thread or pucker the fabric). Hold the garment so you are sewing right to left or bottom to top, whichever is easier. Continue from side to side to about an inch beyond where the seam has ripped. Check the outside of the garment to make sure that no thread is showing. When finished, knot and cut the thread.

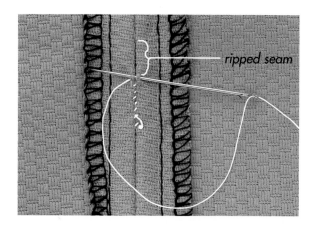

ripped seam

If the seam allowances are difficult to get to (for example, if a lining is sewn to the garment), you can use the slipstitch on the next page on the outside (right side) of the garment. Make sure that the thread color matches and stitches are tiny.

Using a Slipstitch on Heavier Knits

Sewing on the right side of the garment can be done on heavier knits, such as sweaters. Use the "slipstitch" because it will be invisible.

Start from the wrong side to hide the knot. Come up through the seam about 1/2" from the rip. Each stitch goes into the fold, comes out, goes straight across into the opposite fold. This way, when the thread is pulled tight, the thread disappears. Finish by pulling the thread to the wrong side and knotting the thread.

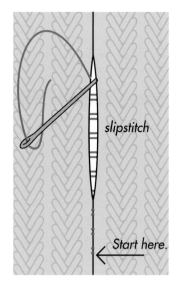

slipstitch

← *Start here.*

Fixing a Crotch Seam

Mending a crotch seam that has begun to pull apart is done in the same manner as any other seam that is ripping.

If you have difficulty getting to the crotch seam, try this: Turn one leg inside out and put the other leg inside of it.

Use the backstitch method with a double thread for extra strength. You might want to go over the ripped portion of the seam twice. Remember to begin about an inch before the rip begins and end about an inch afterward (see page 47). Leave the thread that has pulled out of the seam there if possible. In this way you will not have loose ends to pull out.

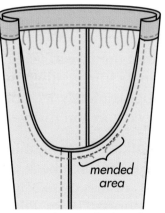

mended area

Put one leg inside the other.

Tip: Cutting the thread, not breaking or biting it, will make a cleaner, sharper end that will be easier to thread through the eye of the needle.

CHAPTER SEVEN:
Fixing Pockets & Linings

Supplies Needed

- ❏ needle
- ❏ thread
- ❏ scissors

Fix a Hole in an Inside Pocket

To fix a hole in an inside pocket, you can use the same backstitch used to fix a ripped seam (see page 46).

Use thread the color of the pocket, which is usually white, off-white, or black.

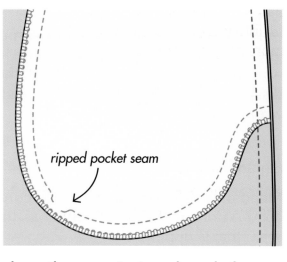

ripped pocket seam

Knot the thread using a single thread. Beginning approximately 1" above or below where the seam is ripped, push the needle in and through to the underside.

Working from right to left, begin by taking a stitch back to the right about 1/8" or less on exactly the same line as the ripped seam. Push the needle back up to the left about 1/4" or less ahead of the previous stitch, moving in the direction of the rip. Continue sewing, each time taking a 1/8" stitch back over the surface of the fabric and then a 1/4" stitch forward under the surface.

Be consistent with your stitching, always keeping the thread on the same side of the needle.

Continue sewing until you are about 1" beyond where the seam is ripped.

Do not pull the thread too tight; you want the resulting seam to be smooth and free of puckers. As always, practice the stitch before you sew your garment.

Finish by knotting the thread. Since the pocket will not show, it does not matter which side of the fabric your knot is on.

Hole in an Inside Pocket

If the pocket has a hole, rather than a ripped seam, you can use iron-on patch fabric or a piece of fabric and fusible web to hold it in place. For more about patches, see Chapter 9.

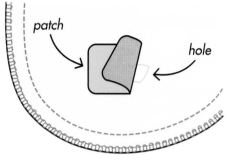

If the hole is close to the seam, you can simply hand sew a deeper seam using the backstitch explained on page 47.

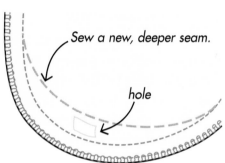

Worn-Out Lining in a Favorite Purse or Tote?

Seams in the linings in purses and totes always seem to wear faster than the outside. Since you can't get to the wrong side of the fabric, repairs to these seams are done differently from other seams. The following technique works for this, as well as for seam repair in pockets in lined pants.

Because the seams are not visible, the stitching can be done on the right side of the lining fabric. Pull the lining or pocket out away from the purse or garment and use an overcast stitch (see page 38) with tiny stitches close together.

CHAPTER EIGHT:
Replacing Elastic

Supplies Needed

- ❏ safety pin
- ❏ elastic
- ❏ needle
- ❏ thread
- ❏ scissors

1. Elastic is encased in a stitched channel called a casing. Rip out the casing stitching for about 2″. Remove the worn-out elastic. Purchase new elastic that is the same width as the old.

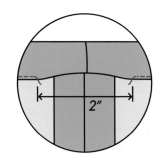

2. Fasten a safety pin to one end of the new elastic and pin the other end to the garment so the elastic doesn't get "lost" in the casing. Thread the elastic through the casing and then overlap the ends and pin together to try on for fitting. Be careful that the elastic does not twist inside the casing.

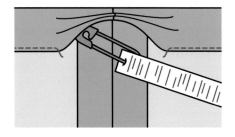

Tip: A device called a Pinch-n-Pull Bodkin is a handy alternative to the safety pin. Look for them in fabric stores.

3. Try on the pants or skirt and repin the elastic until it is comfortable. Lap ends about 1″ and trim off any excess. Hand-sew as shown using a running stitch, working the point of the needle up and down to take up several stitches, then pull the needle through.

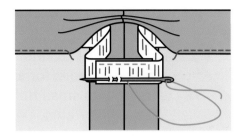

4. Stitch the casing opening closed using a running stitch or backstitch (see page 47), making tiny stitches.

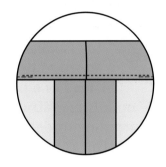

CHAPTER NINE:

Patches

Supplies Needed

❏ needle
❏ thread/yarn
❏ pins
❏ iron-on patch
❏ scissors

Clothes worn often may eventually wear thin, especially the knees of children's pants or the elbows of jackets. An easy fix means that the clothes can be worn for a much longer time. This method is to patch a small hole, usually in play garments, such as denim or khakis—obviously not in dressy clothes, since the patch and stitches will show.

Patching a hole in pants or a jacket is quite simple. Patches come in all shapes and sizes. You do not need to find one that is the same color as the garment. Instead of a patch, you can use a fancy appliqué or decorative upholstery fabric—they all work the same. Also, you can use contrasting thread to sew a patch to look like a design on the garment. This is a great time to use a little creativity.

Patches can be purchased in any sewing or craft store, or even grocery or drug stores. You want iron-on patches or appliqués.

Follow the instructions on the patch/appliqué package. The iron needs to be very hot, so test your garment (on an inside seam) beforehand to make sure it can withstand the hottest iron. Denim is usually fine with the high heat.

There are two methods of patching:

■ On the outside of the garment, over the hole

■ On the inside of the garment, behind the hole

Prepare the Hole/Rip

If the hole has frayed edges, try to cut off some of the threads so the edges are as even as possible.

Prepare the Patch

Trim the patch to about 1/2" larger than the rip/hole all the way around. Since patches usually stay on better if the edges are rounded, cut the patch into a circle or a rectangle with rounded corners. Use items around the house, such as a jar top, to trace the circle.

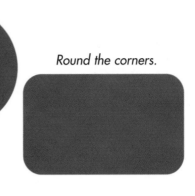

Round the corners.

You do not have to turn under the edges of a purchased patch or appliqué; they will not fray after being ironed down.

Iron On the Patch

Iron the patch onto the outside of the pants. (You can iron the patch onto the inside of the pants; however, with more wear and washings, the hole will probably continue to fray.) Then let the patch cool, since the glue needs to cool to set.

Add Stitching

You can certainly stop once the patch is ironed on. If ironed on properly, the patch should last many washings. However, to secure the patch even better, you may want to stitch around it. This also may give it a decorative look.

Stitch around the patch using the hemming stitch (see pages 38-39). For a decorative look, choose contrasting or decorative thread, such as embroidery thread or thin yarn, and the blanket stitch shown on the next page.

If you use heavier threads, you'll need a larger needle with a large needle eye, such as an embroidery needle.

Decorative/Blanket Stitch

You will sometimes see this stitch on the edges of fleece blankets

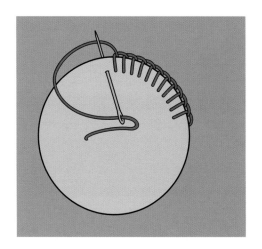

Bring the thread up through the wrong side of the garment to the right side along the edge of the patch. Allowing the thread to form a big loop, as shown, reinsert the needle into both layers at least a 1/4" away from the first stitch and 1/4" into the patch. Bring the needle back out at the edge of the patch, forming a stitch over the edge. Work your way around the patch. When you have sewn completely around the perimeter of the patch, overlap the first few stitches, then pull the needle and thread to the inside of the garment, knot the thread, and cut.

Making Patches from Fashion Fabric and Fusible Web

Though iron-on patches come in an array of fabrics and colors, sometimes what you want is a patch made from fashion fabric. If your fabric can take heat and steam, use a fusible web to adhere it to the portion of your garment where you want or need a patch.

Fusible web is a nylon mesh that melts with the heat of the iron. When put between two layers of fabric, it "glues" them together. It comes in rolls or by the yard.

For small tears, or to reinforce an area on the inside of a garment, lining fabric in a matching color works well.

Cut the patch fabric slightly larger than the area to be covered. Cut fusible web *slightly* smaller than the patch. Remember to round the corners on both.

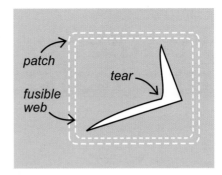

Lay your garment on an ironing board. Place the piece of fusible web over the area to be patched. Cover with the fabric patch, right side up.

Using a steam iron on the steam setting, press the patch for 10-15 seconds. Lift iron and let area cool before moving.

Ravelly Edges?

If your patch fabric ravels, you have two choices for finishing the edges. You can leave the fabric as is, trimming as much of the fraying threads as possible before applying the blanket stitch. But the patch may fray more with each washing. You can try applying Fray Check on the frayed edges before blanket stitching, but first test a small piece of fabric to see how stiff it may get. Let it dry fully before you decide to go ahead. The other choice is to turn under the edges about 1/8"-1/4" around the patch as you sew. If you use this latter method, be sure to cut the patch an extra 1/8"-1/4" larger on all sides before you begin.

CHAPTER TEN:
Fixing Snags in Sweaters

There's no need to get rid of a sweater with a snag! Use a crochet hook and pull the snag through to the inside. (If you do not have a crochet hook, use a larger needle or even a pin or paper clip.)

Put the hook through the sweater fabric at the snag. Catch the loop of the snag and pull the snag to the inside.

outside of sweater

inside of sweater

If the yarn in a snag is broken, tie the two ends together. The knot can be pulled to the inside of the sweater so it won't show.

You've now learned basic mending techniques. Read on for more tips and techniques.

CHAPTER ELEVEN:
Ironing & Pressing Tips

Supplies Needed

❑ iron
❑ press cloth
❑ ironing board or table with a towel

Use a Press Cloth

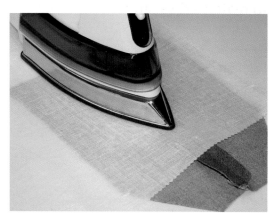

Many fabrics can get shiny from the heat of the iron. To avoid this, the most important thing is to use a press cloth between the iron and the fabric when pressing the right side of the garment. Press cloths are usually special, heat-resistant fabrics or organic fabrics (such as cotton or silk organza), which do not heat up as quickly as the fabric to be ironed. They can be purchased at sewing stores, some grocery stores, or anywhere irons are sold. If you do not have a press cloth, a cotton sheet or pillowcase can be used just as well.

What is the difference between ironing and pressing?

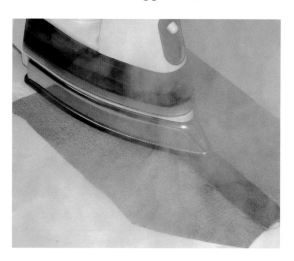

Ironing is moving the iron back and forth to take out wrinkles. The iron is not lifted from the fabric. Pressing is an up and down motion and is used to set fabric so a seam allowance "remembers" to lie flat, or a crease stays in pants. (This works in the same way as curling your hair with heat. When it cools, it stays curled.)

To press a garment, place the iron on the fabric (with press cloth between) and press for a few seconds. Lift, move to the next area to be pressed, and press again. It is easy once you practice a bit.

When sewing, it is good idea to press before and after stitching.

Pressing Pants

The easiest way to crease pants is to match side seams and inseams together and then press (sometimes in wider pants, the back of the pants legs are wider than the fronts, but seams can still be matched up). Press the front crease from the crotch area straight down to the hem. Do the same for the back crease.

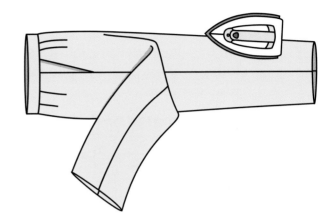

Pressing Popular & Specialty Fabrics

Cotton:

When pressing cotton fabrics, set iron on the "cotton" setting (usually the highest/hottest setting) and use a lot of steam (water in your iron). Spray starch helps get the wrinkles out on crisp cottons. Try a small amount first on the inside of the garment to make sure it does not stain the fabric.

Faux (fake) fur:

For faux furs made with synthetic (manmade) fibers (which 99% are), use an extremely low heat setting without steam and use a thick press cloth, such as a towel.

Fleece:

Fleece has become one of the most popular cool-weather fabrics. Since these fabrics are made from synthetic fibers, most will melt if ironed. If you absolutely must iron a fleece garment, use a very low iron setting and a press cloth. Test a small area first.

Linen:

Linens require a hot iron to remove wrinkles, but they can easily get a shine. Use a steam iron and/or damp press cloth and press from the wrong side. Spray starch can also be used, but always test the spray on a small area to make sure it does not spot.

Nap fabric:

Nap or pile fabrics are fabrics such as corduroys or velvets. Use a terry cloth towel for pressing pile fabrics. Check your iron setting to match fabric content.

Rubber-coated and vinyl fabric:

Use finger pressing to open seams and then glue or stitch seam allowances in place. If pressing is necessary, use a very low setting with a press cloth.

Spandex:

When pressing fabrics with spandex (think stretch), use a low heat setting and a dry iron. Even when the material is combined with cotton or linen, use the lower heat setting. Use steam sparingly. Fabrics with a high percentage of spandex are used mostly for activewear, but a small percentage of spandex (3% to 5%) is now being used in many everyday fabrics as well.

Synthetic (manmade) suede and leather (known as micro-suede):

A dry iron (without water) at a low temperature setting is best for these heat-sensitive fabrics. If the fabric begins to soften and stick to the iron, lower the temperature even more and use a press cloth. Real suede or leather should not be pressed (professional cleaners have special steam machines).

Water-repellent fabrics (such as raincoats):

These fabrics are specially finished to be water-repellent and do not require steam. Water will simply bead and roll off the surface of the fabric. High heat could damage the water-repellent finish. If it is absolutely necessary to press this type of fabric, use the lowest heat setting and a press cloth and test first.

Wool:

Always use a press cloth when working with wool garments. Set the iron on the "wool" setting (slightly lower than the cotton setting) and use a lot of steam. Let the fabric dry before lifting up and hanging; otherwise it may stretch out of shape.

Pressing Troubleshooting

Always Read Your Iron's Instructions

It is important to read the instructions that come with your iron. Some older irons can use distilled water only (it stops the calcium brown spot buildup). Most newer irons can use tap water, or a combination of tap and distilled water. Some should not have distilled water put into them. Also, for many home-use irons, you must empty the water from the iron after each use.

Press Marks

Sometimes when pressing seam allowances, edges will show through on the right side of the garment. The best method to avoid press marks is to place a strip of brown paper (from a grocery bag) between the seam allowance and the fabric.

Hem Imprints

Hem imprints are the marks on the right side of the garment showing the top edge of the hem. When a hem is folded up and pressed into position for sewing, avoid pressing over the edge of the hem allowance, or use brown paper between the hem allowance and the garment wrong side to prevent a hem imprint. (See the photo above using brown paper to prevent seam allowance impressions.)

Scorch Spots

Scorch (burned) spots will look different on different fabrics. With synthetic/manmade fabrics, the scorch spots will look shiny because the fabric is actually slightly melted. Other fabrics may be merely matted down and feel "crispy." Try following solution on a less scorched area. It may not bring the fabric back to normal if it is melted.

Add several drops of household ammonia to a few cups of water. Use a cloth to sponge the scorched area on the garment with this mixture. Rinse well with clean water.

Setting or Removing Creases

Mix equal amounts of white vinegar and water. Apply small amounts directly (using a spray bottle helps) to the fabric and press to set or remove creases.

Dirty Soleplate Print

The soleplate is the flat part of the iron that heats up. A dirty soleplate can leave marks on your garments. Use a nonabrasive cleaning agent recommended for irons (such as Dritz® Iron-Off™ or Rowenta Hot Iron Cleaner, found in sewing or craft supply stores). Follow the directions on the cleaner.

Heat the iron to the highest setting with no water/steam and then unplug. Place a small dab of cleaner on a thick clean cloth or paper towels and rub onto the hot surface. ("Ironing" a clean washcloth works well.) Once the soleplate is clean, use a clean cloth to remove all traces of the cleaner. Use a cotton swab to clean out the steam vents.

Spitting Iron

Lint buildup in the soleplate vents can scorch and cause brown water spotting when the iron is used on the steam setting. If you have a "burst of steam" button, push it a few times before and after each pressing session to help clear the steam vents of lint and minerals (also see instructions for a dirty soleplate).

CHAPTER TWELVE:
Easy Sewing Fashion Tips

Changing/Matching Buttons

Now that you know how to sew on a button, try sewing on decorative buttons to snazz-up the look of a garment. Buttons can be found in almost any crafts or sewing store. Try mix-matching buttons or keep a theme, such as the current holiday. Match the buttons of a jacket to a skirt or pants color for a more coordinated look.

Coats are a great place to change buttons. Many coats come with very plain buttons. Replacing them with decorative buttons can change the whole look of a garment.

Want to Use a Smaller Button?

It is possible when changing buttons to use a smaller one, but the buttonholes will need to be sewn smaller. First, figure out how much smaller the buttonhole needs to be. If the garment is rarely buttoned, then the buttonhole can probably be left at the larger size.

With thread matching the buttonhole thread (usually the same as the garment, but sometimes a contrasting color is used), use the same tiny stitches as in the instructions for fixing Seam D, page 48.

Single thread should be used in lighter-weight garments and double thread should be used in heavier garments, such as jackets or coats.

All stitching will be done from the inside of the garment. Begin at the corner of the buttonhole farthest away from the edge of the garment. Take a tiny stitch of the fabric and go from one side to the other, pulling tight (not too tight to break the thread). Continue from side to side until the

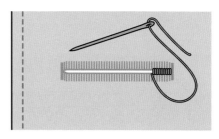

buttonhole is about the right size for the smaller button to fit through comfortably, but snugly. Test several times before knotting and cutting thread. Go over the last few stitches several times, knot off, and cut the thread.

Changing Skirt Lengths as Fashions Change

Skirt lengths sometimes go up and down depending on the mood or the season. If you love the fabric and do not want to get rid of the skirt or dress, try cutting it shorter. Follow the hemming instructions in Chapter Five. No matter what amount you cut off, the process is the same.

Remember, before cutting, measure the garment and try it on to double-check the length. Leave 1½"-2" for the hem allowance.

Comfort Tip:

When mending or sewing, sit up straight and rest the item on your lap (using a pillow if needed) or on a table; do not hold the garment in mid-air to sew. To prevent backache, try not to bend over too much.

Tricks with Trims and Patches

Trims as Camouflage

Use lace appliqués, ribbon, Ultrasuede scraps, or decorative strips to camouflage stains, cigarette burns, or moth holes.

Tip: Average-size needles can be used for almost any fabric, but with very fine fabrics, use a smaller, thinner needle.

Rescue a Jacket

Cover worn jacket elbows with pre-cut leather patches, or cut your own from Ultrasuede® fabric. See Patches, Chapter 9, for how-tos.

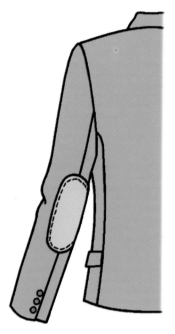

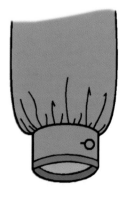

Cover Up a Frayed Cuff Edge on a Blouse or Dress

If the lower edge of a cuff is frayed, add a narrow ribbon or braid trim.

Hand Mending Made Easy

Some Final Encouragement and Extra Little Hints to Help You Along

No one learns to sew in an hour or even a day. Like any skill, it takes practice to become better and more confident.

1. **How can you keep your thread from tangling and knotting when you are hand mending?**

   - Shorten your thread to a length of about 18"- 20".

   - Purchase better thread (cheaper threads tangle more easily).

   - When taking a stitch, pull the needle in the direction you are sewing.

   - Wax your thread by pulling it through beeswax (see page 8). Beeswax can be purchased in most sewing stores.

2. **Why doesn't your garment hang straight and smooth after the new button/snap is sewn on and the garment is buttoned/snapped?**

   - The button was probably not sewn in the correct place. Unbutton the button in question and let the garment hang naturally. Place a pin through the buttonhole. Does it mark a spot different from where your button was sewn? Even a tiny change will make a big difference in how a garment hangs on the body.

   - If a snap has recently been replaced, the same response holds. The exact position for a snap is a bit more difficult to locate, but review the steps in Chapter Four and re-mark the exact location for the snap. Is it different from where you sewed the snap on?

3. **Why won't the new button go through the buttonhole?**

   The button is probably too large or too thick. Replace it with a slightly smaller or thinner one. When buying a new button(s), take the old one or the garment with you to the store for sizing. Buttonholes are sewn to match the size of the button.

4. **Why is the thread showing through on the right side of the garment when you mend a ripped seam?**

   Two things could be occurring. Make sure that you are stitching exactly on the old stitching line. Make sure that your stitches are tiny and tight. Also, try changing the color of the thread to a shade slightly darker than the fabric.

5. **How do you get your stitches even?**

   Practice!
   Practice!
   Practice!

CONGRATULATIONS!

You now know how to hand mend
almost any type of garment.

Think of the time and money you will be saving by not taking
garments to the tailor's, dropping them off, picking them up,
or searching for replacement garments because something
needs to be fixed.

Doesn't it feel great to know that you can
now do this yourself?

When Not to Try to Fix Your Garment

Mending and sewing are skills that have many levels. Simple hand mending can be learned with a little practice. However, alterations and other sewing techniques take years of learning and experience. Even with this book, there may be instances when you should take your garment to a tailor (such as at your local dry cleaners) to be mended or fixed.

Some of these instances may be:

■ Mending a seam that has a zipper.

■ Replacing a zipper.

■ Mending a hole or tear where a patch cannot, or should not, be used (the hole is too large, the heat needed to iron on the patch cannot be used on the garment fabric, etc.).

■ Hemming very fine fabrics, such as chiffon or silk. Usually a special hem done by machine or hand (called a rolled hem) is used.

■ The ripped seam is too large/long to do by hand (usually more than 2″ or so).

■ Several cross seams have ripped (such as the underarm and sleeve seams together).

■ Buttonholes have ripped through to the fabric.

■ Darning socks. Unless you just can't bring yourself to throw a pair of socks away, darning or fixing holes in socks is not really worth the time. Many socks are inexpensive and darning is a long process.

One Last Comment

If you do decide to discard any garment
—if it is in wearable condition—
please donate it to a local charity.

Charity names and contact information
can be found in your local phone book
(check under nonprofit or
not-for-profit organizations).

INDEX

The Basic Hand Stitches

This book covers these basic
hand-mending stitches:

Backstitch (pg. 46)

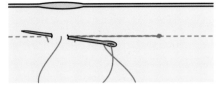

Designer Hem Stitch (pg. 40)

Decorative/Blanket Stitch (pg. 56)

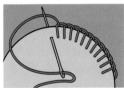

Overcast Stitch (pg. 38)

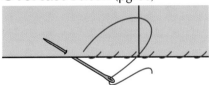

Running Stitch (pg. 18)

Slipstitch (pg. 39, 49)

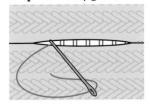

Sewing Products Available from Palmer/Pletsch Publishing

Books available coil bound—add $3 for large books, $2 for small.

Would you like to learn to sew better? Look for these easy-to-use, information-filled sewing books and videos in local book and fabric stores, or visit our website to order:

www.palmerpletsch.com

LARGE FORMAT BOOKS:
Bridal Gowns *160 pgs.,$19.95*
The BUSINE$$ of Teaching Sewing *128 pgs., $29.95*
Couture—The Art of Fine Sewing *208 pgs., $29.95*
Creative Home Decorating Ideas *160 pgs., $19.95*
Dream Sewing Spaces *128 pgs., $19.95*
Fit For Real People *256 pgs., $24.95*
Jackets For Real People *128 pgs., $24.95*
Looking Good *160 pgs., $19.95*
Pants For Real People *176 pgs., $24.95*
Sewing Ultrasuede® Brand Products *128 pgs., $16.95*
Théâtre de la Mode *192 pgs., $29.95*

SMALL FORMAT BOOKS:
Easy, Easier, Easiest Tailoring *128 pgs., $9.95*
Creative Serging *128 pgs., $9.95*
Hand Mending Made Easy *80 pgs., $14.95*
Mother Pletsch's Painless Sewing *128 pgs., $9.95*
Pants For Any Body *128 pgs., $8.95*
Sewing With Sergers *128 pgs., $9.95*
Sew To Success! *128 pgs., $10.95*
Smart Packing *240 pgs., $19.95*
The Shade Book *144 pgs., $11.95*

DVDs — *$19.95 each*
Serger Basics
Creative Serging
21st Century Sewing
Fit for Real People: Basics
Learn to Sew a Shirt
   or Blouse
Looking Good, Live!
Pants for Real People:
   Fitting Techniques
Pants for Real People:
   Sewing Techniques
Sew an Ultrasuede Jacket
Sewing...Good to Great: It's in the Details
Jackets for Real People—
   $24.95 (2¾ hrs.)
Perfect Fusing—*$14.95*

*We also offer workshops, teacher training, **Perfect Sew Wash-Away Fabric Stabilizer, Perfect Pattern Paper**, plus additional products for children and teachers.*

Needle Threader
for hand and machine needles.
$4.50

PerfectFUSE INTERFACING
Available in 1-yard and 3-yard packages:
PerfectFuse SHEER *$7.95/$23.50*
PerfectFuse LIGHT *$7.95/$23.50*
PerfectFuse MEDIUM *$8.95/$26.50*
PerfectFuse TAILOR *$12.95/$38.50*

Perfect WAISTBANDS
1" x 5 yds: $4.00

Take A Sewing Vacation!

Palmer/Pletsch
1801 N.W. Upshur St, Suite 100 Portland, OR 97209
(503) 274-0687   ORDERS: 1-800-728-3784
www.palmerpletsch.com

Do you know a young child who would like to learn to sew?

My First Sewing Books, *by Winky Cherry,* are available packaged as kits with materials for a first project. With a Teaching Manual & Video, they offer a complete, thoroughly tested sewing program for young children, 5 to 11 years old. They'll learn patience, manners, creativity, completion, and how to follow rules— all through the enjoyment of sewing. Each book follows a project from start to finish with clever rhymes and clear illustrations. *Each book, 8½" x 8½", 40 pages*

HAND SEWING SERIES
each book alone $10.95
book with kit $14.95

My First Sewing Book
Children as young as five can learn to hand sew and stuff a felt bird shape. Also available in Spanish.

My First Embroidery Book
Beginners learn the importance of accuracy by making straight stitches and using a chart and gingham to make a name sampler.

My First Doll Book
Felt dolls have embroidered faces, yarn hair, and clothes. Children use the overstitch and skills learned in Levels I and II.

MACHINE SEWING SERIES
each book alone $10.95
book with kit $12.95

My First Machine Sewing Book
With practice pages, then a fabric star, children learn about the machine, seam allowances, tapering, snips, clips and stitching and turning a shape right side out.

My First Patchwork Book
Children use a template to make a fourpatch block and can make the entire alphabet of patchwork flags used by sailors, soldiers, pilots, and astronauts.

My First Quilt Book
Children machine stitch a quilt pieced with strips and squares and finish it with yarn ties or optional hand quilting.

TEACHING MATERIALS

Teaching Children to Sew Manual and Video, *$29.95*
The 112-page, 8½" x 11"
Teaching Manual shows you exactly how to teach young children, including preparing the environment, workshop space, class control, and the importance of incorporating other life skills along with sewing skills. In the **DVD Video** *(1 hour)*, see Winky Cherry teach six 6-to-8-year olds how to sew in a true-life classroom setting. She introduces herself and explains the rules, then shows them how to sew. Then, see close-ups of a child sewing the project in double-time. (Show this to your students.) Finally, Winky gives you a tour of an ideal classroom setup. She also talks about the tools, patterns and sewing supplies you will need.

Teacher's Supplies
Additional kit supplies, patterns and teaching materials for **The Winky Cherry System of Sewing** are available. Call for a catalog.

About the Author of
Hand Mending Made Easy

Nan Ides comes from a family who always sewed. When she was growing up, her home always had a sewing box and sewing machine threaded and ready to use. She was shocked when she became aware of how much others paid for simple mending jobs, such as replacing a button or hemming a garment.

Ms. Ides' goal is to teach as many people as she can to do simple mending jobs themselves—to save money and time, and for self-satisfaction.

While Ms. Ides has a formal business background, with a B.A. in Psychology and an M.S. in Information Management, she has also been sewing for most of her life, designing many of her own clothes. This passion has led her to study with nationally known designers and sewing instructors.

Being petite, Nan always had to hem or shorten her clothes. Sometimes it was just easier to make her own clothes. Her teaching experience began when people asked her to sew on a button for them. Instead, Nan would respond. "I'll charge you $10 to sew on the button, or I'll teach you how to do it for free."

Nan now teaches hand mending for several community groups in the Philadelphia, Pennsylvania, area. For more information on group classes, she may be reached at mendingbook@earthlink.net.